SPOTLIGHT ON EARTH SCIENCE

MOUNTAINS AND CANYONS

DENNIS RUDENKO

PowerKiDS

NEW YORK

Published in 2017 by The Rosen Publishing Group, Inc.
29 East 21st Street, New York, NY 10010

Editor: Caitie McAneney
Book design: Michael Flynn
Interior layout: Reann Nye

Photo Credits: Cover John E Marriott/All Canada Photos/Getty Images; p. 4 Lucky-photographer/Shutterstock.com; p. 5 Anton_Ivanov/Shutterstock.com; p. 7 f11photo/Shutterstock.com; p. 9 Kevin Schafer/age fotostock/ Getty Images; p. 10 Bettmann/Getty Images; p. 11 Anton Rogozin/Shutterstock.com; p. 13 Kjersti Joergensen/ Shutterstock.com; pp. 14, 19 Rafal Cichawa/Shutterstock.com; p. 15 Asif Islam/Shutterstock.com; p. 16 Bill Hatcher/ National Geographic/Getty Images; p. 17 prochasson frederic/Shutterstock.com; p. 21 Jason Edwards/National Geographic/Getty Images; p. 22 Janis Maleckis/Shutterstock.com.

Cataloging-in-Publication Data

Names: Rudenko, Dennis.
Title: Mountains and canyons / Dennis Rudenko.
Description: New York : PowerKids Press, 2017. | Series: Spotlight on earth science | Includes index.
Identifiers: ISBN 9781499425277 (pbk.) | ISBN 9781499425307 (library bound) | ISBN 9781499425284 (6 pack)
Subjects: LCSH: Mountains--Juvenile literature. | Canyons--Juvenile literature.
Classification: LCC GB512.R83 2017 | DDC 551.4'32--d23

Manufactured in China

CPSIA Compliance Information: Batch #BW17PK For further information contact Rosen Publishing, New York, New York at 1-800-237-9932.

CONTENTS

AMAZING LANDFORMS 4

MANY KINDS OF MOUNTAINS 6

TECTONIC PLATES 8

WORLD'S BIGGEST 10

UNDERWATER MOUNTAINS 12

CREATING CANYONS 14

THE GRAND CANYON 16

WORLD'S DEEPEST 18

SUBMARINE CANYONS 20

THINK LIKE AN EARTH SCIENTIST 22

GLOSSARY 23

INDEX 24

PRIMARY SOURCE LIST 24

WEBSITES 24

CHAPTER ONE

AMAZING LANDFORMS

Mountains have some of the highest **elevations** on Earth's surface, while canyons have some of the lowest depths. They are both considered landforms, or natural features of the earth. Without landforms, Earth's surface would be flat and boring. Mountains and canyons are the peaks and dips that make the world's **landscapes** exciting and different.

ANTELOPE CANYON, ARIZONA

Machu Picchu is a famous ancient city that was built by the Inca people in the Andes Mountains in Peru. Many people hike through the mountains to see this amazing view.

Have you ever seen a mountain? They are large, steep hills. Many are so tall they can be seen from miles away. Some mountains stand alone, while others are part of huge groups called mountain ranges. Two well-known mountain ranges are the Rocky Mountains and the Himalayas.

Canyons are narrow, deep valleys. They're surrounded by steep cliffs. They sometimes look like gashes in Earth's surface. Scientists have also found canyons deep in the ocean. Read on to learn more about mountains and canyons!

CHAPTER TWO

MANY KINDS OF MOUNTAINS

Did you know there's more than one kind of mountain? They're all huge landforms made mostly of rock, but they're formed in different ways.

Some mountains are volcanic. They were formed when hot, liquid rock called lava **erupted** through Earth's surface. It cooled, hardened, and built up in one spot, eventually becoming a mountain. Volcanic mountains may still be active and can let out ash or lava. Mount Saint Helens is a famously active volcanic mountain in the state of Washington.

Dome mountains are formed when magma pushes against Earth's surface layer, but doesn't erupt. The magma hardens and gives the landform a rounded shape, or a dome. The Black Hills in South Dakota are good examples of dome mountains.

Plateau mountains are flat-topped areas of high elevation. The land was pushed upward by underground **tectonic plate** movement, and **erosion** gave it a flattened top.

Fault-block mountains form along faults, or cracks in Earth's surface. The crust comes apart and blocks of rock drop down or are pushed up. These Sierra Nevada mountains are fault-block mountains.

CHAPTER THREE

TECTONIC PLATES

Major landforms on Earth were created by plate tectonics. Some people think the planet's surface is solid all the way around. In reality, this surface, which is called the lithosphere, is broken into large slabs called tectonic plates. Because they float on a layer of partly melted rock, they're always in motion.

There are a few ways tectonic plates can interact with each other. Some have a divergent boundary, which means two plates move away from each other. On land, this causes deep valleys. In the ocean, two diverging plates can cause underwater mountains. As the plates pull apart, magma rises to the seafloor, hardens, and builds into mountains.

Convergent boundaries are places where tectonic plates move towards each other. If the plates collide under the land, the crust may rise and form a mountain. When oceanic plates collide, one plate often dives underneath the other. This forms a deep, narrow trench.

When two plates grind past each other, it's called a transform boundary. An example is the San Andreas Fault in California. These moving plates can cause huge earthquakes.

CHAPTER FOUR

WORLD'S BIGGEST

Mount Everest is the highest mountain on Earth. This mountain is located along the boundary between Tibet and Nepal. It's part of the Himalayas. Mount Everest is more than 29,000 feet (8,839.2 m) tall. Some of the world's best mountain climbers have attempted the climb. The first people to reach Mount Everest's **summit** were explorer Sir Edmund Hillary and a **Sherpa** named Tenzing Norgay in 1953.

TENZING NORGAY   SIR EDMUND HILLARY

People who climb Mount Everest face sickness due to the very high **altitude**. The summit is in the "death zone," which is a height range at which humans can only survive for a few days.

Mount Everest may be the world's highest mountain, but it's not the tallest mountain. Mount Everest has the highest elevation *above* **sea level**. Mauna Kea, which is located in Hawaii, is actually the tallest mountain in the world, but its base is far below the ocean's surface. This huge mountain begins at the bottom of the Pacific Ocean and rises out of the water. It's more than 33,500 feet (10,210.8 m) tall when you measure it from base to peak.

CHAPTER FIVE

UNDERWATER MOUNTAINS

The ocean is full of its own mountain peaks. Underwater mountains are sometimes called seamounts or submarine mountains. Scientists can map these underwater mountains and mountain ranges using sonar. Sonar is a system for finding underwater objects by sending out a series of sounds and measuring how long it takes them to echo back.

When people think of long mountain ranges, they often think of the Andes, the Himalayas, or the Rocky Mountains. However, the longest mountain range on Earth is actually underwater. The mid-ocean ridge system stretches for nearly 40,400 miles (65,017.5 km). The mid-ocean ridge system is located along a huge tectonic plate boundary. When the plates pulled apart, magma rose to the seafloor surface and hardened. Over time, this formed a huge system of underwater mountains that stretch nearly all the way around the globe.

Thingvellir National Park in Iceland is home to one of the few above-water parts of the Mid-Atlantic Ridge, which is part of the mid-ocean ridge system.

CHAPTER SIX

CREATING CANYONS

Canyons are created very differently from mountains. River canyons are usually formed when flowing water wears through rock. This is a long process of erosion. Rivers travel from higher elevations to elevations that are level with a larger body of water for **drainage**. The energy of the flowing water cuts through rock over time, creating a canyon.

Just as there are different kinds of mountains, there are

COLCA CANYON, PERU

Canyons are often found in dry places. Dry places lend themselves well to erosion by wind and water.

different kinds of canyons. Slot canyons are thin channels that have been cut into plateaus by flowing water. These canyons can be hundreds of feet deep and only a few feet across. Slot canyons often form in **porous** rocks, such as sandstone and limestone. Utah has many slot canyons.

Box canyons are created when water is absorbed into the porous rocks of cliffs. Parts of the cliff walls cave in, forming a canyon with cliffs on three sides.

CHAPTER SEVEN

THE GRAND CANYON

The Grand Canyon is one of the most breathtaking landforms on Earth. This amazing canyon is nearly 277 miles (445.8 km) long and up to 18 miles (29 km) wide. Most of the canyon's bottom is around 1 mile (1.6 km) below sea level, but the depth varies.

The Grand Canyon is located in the U.S. state of Arizona. The canyon was formed by the Colorado River. This river still flows through the canyon at about 4 miles (6.4 km) per hour.

This canyon has a unique **ecosystem**. The weather is often very hot and dry. It's home to hundreds of mammal, reptile, and bird species. **Artifacts** found in the Grand Canyon show that people have lived in the area for nearly 12,000 years. Today, you can visit Grand Canyon National Park to see this huge canyon for yourself.

Scientists think it took between 3 million and 6 million years for erosion to create the Grand Canyon.

CHAPTER EIGHT

WORLD'S DEEPEST

The Grand Canyon may be one of the most famous canyons, but it's not the deepest. The deepest canyon in the United States is actually Hells Canyon. This canyon is located in parts of Idaho, Washington, and Oregon. The rushing waters of the Snake River created it. At its deepest point, it's 7,993 feet (2,436.3 m) from the canyon floor to the cliff peak. That's about 1.5 miles (2.4 km)!

Not even Hells Canyon is the deepest canyon in the world. Many give that title to Cotahuasi Canyon in southwestern Peru. It's twice as deep as the Grand Canyon! At its deepest point, it's about 11,000 feet (3,352.8 m) from the canyon floor to the cliff peak. That's more than 2 miles (3.2 km) deep! Other people consider the Yarlung Tsangpo Grand Canyon in Tibet or the Kali Gandaki Gorge in Nepal to be the deepest canyons in the world.

This picture shows a portion of the Cotahuasi Canyon in Peru.

CHAPTER NINE

SUBMARINE CANYONS

Just as there are mountains underwater, there are also canyons underwater. These submarine canyons look a lot like land canyons. Submarine canyons are often formed by ocean currents flowing along the seafloor. These currents wear away at the rocky floor over time, creating a canyon with steep walls.

One of the deepest submarine canyons ever discovered is the Great Bahama Canyon. This canyon drops more than 14,000 feet (4,267.2 m) from the seafloor to its deepest point. It's at least more than 140 miles (225.3 km) long, but scientists think it could be even longer.

In 2015, scientists traveled to Perth Canyon, which is off the coast of western Australia. They wanted to explore this underwater canyon, which is about the size of the Grand Canyon. They found steep cliffs, pitch-dark depths, and deep-sea creatures living on the canyon walls.

Humans have only explored a small part of the ocean, so deeper canyons surely exist!

CHAPTER TEN

THINK LIKE AN EARTH SCIENTIST

People travel from around the world to visit the Grand Canyon in Arizona or to climb Mount Everest. For some, visiting such a landform is a once-in-a-lifetime opportunity! Luckily, many mountains and canyons are part of national parks. That makes them even easier to explore.

Mountains and canyons aren't formed overnight. They take millions of years to become the landforms you see today. Canyons form little by little as water rushes against rock. Mountains grow taller as tectonic plates collide. The mountains of the mid-ocean ridge system expand as tectonic plates pull apart, and magma rushes up to the cold, deep seafloor.

Next time you see a mountain or canyon, ask yourself: How did this structure form? What forces caused this to happen? How long did this take? Think like an earth scientist and you may find the answers to your questions!

GLOSSARY

altitude (AL-tuh-tood) The height of something above a certain level.

artifact (AHR-tih-fakt) Something made by humans in the past that still exists.

drainage (DRAY-nehj) The act or process of removing water from a place.

ecosystem (EE-koh-sih-stuhm) All the living things in an area.

elevation (eh-luh-VAY-shun) The height of a place above the level of the sea.

erosion (ih-ROH-shun) The process by which something is worn away by natural forces, such as water and wind.

erupt (ih-RUHPT) Burst forth.

landscape (LAND-skayp) An area of land that has a certain appearance or quality.

porous (POH-ruhs) Having small holes that allow air or liquid to pass through.

sea level (SEE LEH-vuhl) The average height of the sea's surface.

Sherpa (SHUR-puh) A member of the Sherpa people of the Himalayas. Often hired to help guide mountain climbers.

summit (SUH-miht) The top of a mountain.

tectonic plate (tehk-TAH-nihk PLAYT) One of the moveable masses of rock that create Earth's surface.

INDEX

A
Andes Mountains, 5, 12

B
Black Hills, 6
box canyons, 15

C
Colca Canyon, 14
Colorado River, 16
Cotahuasi Canyon, 18, 19
convergent boundaries, 8

D
divergent boundary, 8
dome mountains, 6

F
fault-block mountains, 7

G
Grand Canyon, 16, 17, 18,
    20, 22
Great Bahama Canyon, 20

H
Hells Canyon, 18
Hillary, Sir Edmund, 10, 11
Himalayas, 5, 10, 12

K
Kali Gandaki Gorge, 18

M
Machu Picchu, 5
Mauna Kea, 10
Mid-Atlantic Ridge, 12
mid-ocean ridge system, 12,
    22
Mount Everest, 10, 11, 22
Mount Saint Helens, 6

N
Norgay, Tenzing, 10, 11

P
Pacific Ocean, 10
Perth Canyon, 20
plateau mountains, 6

R
river canyon, 14
Rocky Mountains, 5, 12

S
San Andreas Fault, 9
seamounts, 12
Sierra Nevada, 7
slot canyons, 15
Snake River, 18

T
transform boundary, 9

V
volcanic mountains, 6

Y
Yarlung Tsangpo Grand
    Canyon, 18

PRIMARY SOURCE LIST

Page 5
Machu Picchu. Built by the Inca people in the mid-1400s. Stone. Located in the Cusco region of Peru.

Page 10
Sir Edmund Hillary and Tenzing Norgay are shown after their successful climb of Mount Everest. Black-and-white photograph. 1953. Taken by Peter Jackson, Reuters.

Page 16
Pictographs of bighorn sheep, deer, and human figures. Drawings on stone. Found in the western region of Grand Canyon National Park, Arizona. From National Geographic.

WEBSITES

Due to the changing nature of Internet links, PowerKids Press has developed an online list of websites related to the subject of this book. This site is updated regularly. Please use this link to access the list: www.powerkidslinks.com/soes/mount